Graced
FOR IT
DEVOTIONAL
- VOLUME 1 -

Your Purpose Matters

COMPILED BY
CHANTEA M. WILLIAMS

Graced For It Devotional, Volume 1 : Your Purpose Matters
Copyright © 2020 Compiled by Chantea M Williams.

All rights reserved. Printed in the United States of America. No part of this book may be used or reproduced in any manner whatsoever without written permission except in the case of brief quotations em- bodied in critical articles or reviews.

Published by :
Relentless Publishing House, LLC
www.relentlesspublishing.com

ISBN: 978-1-948829-54-0

First Edition: April 2020

10   9 8 7 6 5 4 3 2 1

Co-Authors

Cherie Barnes
Dr. Jennifer Boyer
Ronda Braden
Debbie Cook
Jelisa Cook
Georgette Cunningham
Louis Davis
Tameka Garrett
LaQuetia Gilliard
Antoinette Holman
Jana Jackson
Sharolyn Jackson-Douglas
Javion James
Nakia Morgan
Calotta Porterfield
Tanya E. Randall
Stephanie Sherer
Gloria Strauthers
Sherrie Truelove
Chantal Flax-Ward
Tamika S. Washington
Irene Watson
Dr. Annette West
Keywana West
Jennifer Gray-Wymbs
Chantea M. Williams

Table of Contents

Introduction	7
Finding Purpose Through Your Identity	9
Discovering Purpose: A Deeper Look	11
You Already Have It	13
Persevere Through the Detours	19
Your Purpose is Intentional	23
Stir the Gift	25
Girl You Got This	29
Surrender It All	33
We Are Better Together	35
A Heartful Purpose	39
Do It Afraid	41
Best of Both Worlds, His Strength	43
Change Your Regimen	47
Persevere on Purpose	49
Me Finding Me	53
Transformed Wholeness in God	57
Love From the Inside Out	61
Put Doubt Out	65

In Times of Trouble Say…	69
A Life With Grace and Mercy	73
In Between the Wait	77
The Other Side of Pain	79
Death is Not the End	81
The Purpose Walk	85
Queen Up	89
No More Hustling, Just Chase After God	93
Meet the Authors	97

You have to believe in yourself!

Introduction

" The greatest tragedy in life is not death, but a life without a purpose."

~ Dr. Myles Munroe

Did you read the quote above or did you skip over it? Read it again and this time say it out loud. Does it not make you think if your life is in a current tragedy because you are not living out your purpose? The grave is the wealthies place on earth becaseu many people have died and never fulfilled their purpose or even sought it out. It's almost if they died twice.

Purpose is that thing that keeps you dreaming of the wonderful possibilities that could occur in your life. Purpose is that thing that keeps you tossing and turning at night because there is so much to get done but it doesn't seem like you have enough time. Purpose is given to everyone but not everyone will choose live a life of purpose. Yes, it is your choice whether or not you purposefully.

One thing I have come to find out in my own life, when I choose to walk in purpose, I also live in peace. Think about that statement for a minute. Are you currently living out your purpose? There are many things that we are gifted to do but are those things connected to our purpose?

In this book, we take you a purpose journey. We share our failures and successes. We give you advice based on our own experiences, in hopes that it will help you on your own purpose journey. We want you to know that *Your Purpose Matters* just as much as the next person. It is also your responsibility to make sure you do what you were created to do. You are not to be a carbon copy of others. You are an original! You are unique!

We pray that you are encouraged, empowered and equipped to walk in your purpose unapologetically!

-Chantea M. Williams

Finding Purpose Through Your Identity

For we are God's handiwork, created in Christ Jesus to do good works, which God prepared in advance for us to do.

Ephesians 2:10 NIV

As an individual, and especially a woman, the question of one's purpose can be a reoccurring one. What is my purpose? Have I achieved it? And if I did, was it done well? We feel an innate desire to become someone or something, both personally and professionally, resolute in our belief that we are created for more.

While we exist to fulfil a purpose, finding the point of our lives can be an invigorating, yet daunting task. Yet, when we discover our identity in whose we are, establishing the aim of our lives becomes a less difficult quest. Let your assurance be found in knowing that the God who created you made you in His image and calls you 'His handiwork'.

Oftentimes, it is too easy to question the descriptions that God has given to us. How could I be a *masterpiece*? What about me is *royal* or *special*? These words don't apply to me,' we think to ourselves. After all, there are so many instances in our lives where we feel less than – less than attractive, intelligent or purposeful. The qualities that we identify with have been influenced and shaped by so many other factors and the more negative those attributes, the less we believe in our value and the more inclined we are to accept that we are unworthy for the purpose for which we have been called.

Regardless of our past, age or skill, God has use for each and every one of us. We have all been made on purpose to do greater works. Yet, it is only when we find and embrace our identity in Him that our whole perspective changes to accept and yield to the calling on our lives that He reveals. It is through God's great love for us (v.4) and His saving grace (v.5) that we are able to assume this new self - to be who He says we are and to walk confidently into the purpose for which we have been made.

God has already predestined the purpose for our lives - He has prepared work for us to do in advance – and He has equipped us to accomplish the task. Any belief to the contrary is set out solely to dissuade and distract us from achieving our goal. To find our true meaning in life, we must first accept our true identity as *God's elect*. Once we acknowledge this, the pursuit of our purpose is no longer our search but an opportunity to be discovered through our surrendered self.

Prayer

Almighty Father, thank you for creating me on purpose for a purpose. You word says that I am Your masterpiece, fearfully and wonderfully made, the apple of Your eyes, royal and Your special possession, more than a conqueror, and purposeful. Sometimes I find these qualities hard to embrace because this world has attempted to tell me who I am and that does not always align with who You made me to be. I am grateful for the mercy and saving grace that You have extended to me. As I step out in hopes of finding my purpose, I ask that You help me to embrace this newness of life that You offer - to accept who You say I am - to believe that I am of the utmost value because You made me, that I may boldly step forth into the purpose for which I am called. Renew my mind that I may surrender fully to you and discern Your perfect will for my life. In Jesus' name, I pray. Amen.

Chantal Flax-Ward

Walk in Purpose
Live in Peace

Discovering Purpose: A Deeper Look

And we know [with great confidence] that God [who is deeply concerned about us] causes all things to work together [as a plan] for good for those who love God, to those who are called according to His plan and purpose.

Romans 8:28 AMP

Many people search for purpose in various ways through people, careers, achievement, education, etc. It is often tied to our identity. When people look at you, what do they see? Who are you? I thought I found it, but I didn't. Searching for purpose caused me to take a deeper look and ask myself, "Am I living in my purpose or someone else's?"

I thought about what others have said my purpose should be and remember the times I accepted it. I lacked confidence to look within myself but relied on other's opinions and my accomplishments. Whenever I followed my own way and it seemed that things were not working out as expected, I was haunted by the words others and of their suggestions.

I thought, "This isn't working because this person said I should be doing this instead." I tried it their way and I was not fulfilled. Looking back, their suggestions were based on their acceptance of me into their lives and was rooted in self-fulfillment rather than influencing others. In the end, no matter how hard I tried, I never gained the acceptance I thought I wanted.

Discovering purpose meant I needed to take a much deeper look into myself. What do I like? What am I passionate about? What fulfills me? It took some time and deep soul searching, but the more I began to heal and gain confidence, that is where I began to find it. My purpose was no longer about me, my identity, or anything selfish to gain acceptance from others. It is there where I found freedom.

With a new perspective as I reflect over my life, I can see how God has intricately woven my experiences, successes, failures, and searching, to create a beautiful road map to help others.

Lord forgive me for relying on my own strength and not allowing You to use my pain to discover my purpose in You. Thank You for loving me through my weakness and for working ALL things out for my good and for the good of others. In Jesus name, amen!

Jana Jackson

You Already Have It

By his divine power, God has given us everything we need for living a godly life. We have received all of this by coming to know him, the one who called us to himself by means of his marvelous glory and excellence.

2 Peter 1:3 NLT

We often search for what we need to define, supply, and launch our purpose from outside of ourselves. During our lives, we believe that if we matriculate through the right school, university, gain prestigious certifications, or network with the right people we will achieve our purpose in life. We can by participating in these activities gain skills and even elevation in life. However, we do so without considering if the methods are God ordained. The truth is all that we stand in need of, desire, and dream for what is already inside of us. Before the foundation of the world every skill and ability needed to fulfill our purpose was divinely downloaded into us by God Himself.

I spent much of my early adult years concentrating on what was outside of me believing that people and status was needed to find and fulfill purpose in life. Days and months were spent searching for the right organization containing prestigious people who could "give a good reference". Books were bought or checked out of the library on every related area of interest. Then there was the networking, networking, networking, and networking to develop the art of "working the room". The goal during every event was to make sure you got in front of the right people. Often the goal was achieved and opportunities were successful. Then there were other times it was not, and even hurtful. I was not the only one trying to get ahead. There were also others, often at my expense, leaving me in their wake still empty of purpose and broken. There is nothing worst than seeking to fulfill your purpose only to find a void still remains.

So why was there still a void? We have accomplished the level of education we desired, landed the dream job and living in the dream location. For some of us on top of that we have married the love of our lives. Yet still deep inside the woman who we see is not standing up in victory at the top of the mountain, but instead we see her tear stained face, screaming for something of more substance to fill the void. She needs and deserves a life of purpose. Out of all the steps taken there must be something that is still missing, a path that has not been walked and completed.

The one important step missing that is needed to bring

contentment, and come into our God ordained purpose is God's direction. He's the architect of life. His is the relationship needed to fill the void, and bring clarity to what I was creating. The education, skills, and yes the people we have met through networking were all a part of Gods plan, used to propel me into His purpose for my life. By having faith in God and His ordained plan, we learn we must accept that "everything we need for living a godly life" we already have. Our purpose matters to God because we matter.

Prayer

Heavenly Father, I now acknowledge that before the foundation of the world You have already provided me with everything I need to fulfill my ordained purpose in the earth. Everything that pertains to life and godliness is provided. Forgive me for all the times I depended on education, and others to produce what You have already provided. Forgive me for taking every lesson learned, every experience lived and every dream as if I designed it myself. God give me the strength to trust every gift You have place in me to be a blessing to others. Starting in this moment I receive by faith through an intimate relationship with You God, every opportunity and the paths that you have ordained. By You God, every need is met, every assignment is accomplished and each life touched will be blessed in You. I pray and believe it all in Your Son Jesus name, amen.

Calotta Porterfield

My purpose was predestined before the foundation of the world so I must do the work to seek what it is.

Persevere Through the Detours

Perseverance

Persistence is doing something despite difficulty or delay in achieving success.

So do not throw away your confidence; it will be richly rewarded. You need to persevere so that when you have done the will of God, you will receive what he has promised.

Hebrews 10:35-36 NIV

As a child, I possessed a champion's heart. Which meant I was ready to go to battle, no matter the circumstance or the outcome. I believed I could win. So naturally, I was always on the cusp of circumventing my parents. If you would have told me this attribute is what would get me through some of the darkest moments of my life, I'd say you were foolish. As this personality trait always landed me in hot water with my parents.

This persona would be tested. In 1990, I became a teenage mother and joined the estimated 521,626 births to girls between the ages of 15-19. My family shunned me. Moreover, I harbored the secret of being molested by a family member, which led me to conceal the pain with more sex.

This secret caused my life to spiral out of control. Out of the chaos, and in the deepest valley, arose a scripture Jeremiah 29:11. It says, "God knows the plans he has for us. These plans are designed to prosper us and not to harm us, and these plans guarantee you a hope and a future." My expected end wasn't just to be a statistic, and becoming a teenage mother was only a detour and not a dead-end.

Perhaps today, you've found yourself on a detour. I want to encourage you not to lose heart. The path to your Purpose is often not a straight line. Napoleon Hill says, "You are the master of your destiny. You can influence, direct, and control your environment. You can make your life what you want it to be."

These words caused a paradigm shift. I began to visualize my destiny. When those around me began to doubt my future, I'd always recall Mother Alice Jeter, my Sunday school teacher. She assigned us scriptures to memorize at an earlier age. My scripture was Hebrews 10:35-36 NIV "So do not throw away your confidence; it will be richly rewarded. You need to persevere so that when you have done the will of God, you will receive what he has promised." That is what motivated me to get back on my Purpose journey. Glory to God! Because I persevered through the detour, I went on to graduate from high school with honors, and I received a scholarship to college. To me, that was my reward for perseverance.

This reward is just one example of how perseverance results in a reward. Today, you may find yourself in hardship or a detour waiting to see the light at the end of the tunnel or a clear path. Remember, there will always be a reward at the end of a detour if you persevere.

Prayer:

Father, thank You for knowing the plans that You have for me. Please help me to understand that detours are a part of my Purpose, and they exist only to build character and strengthen my Faith. Please help me to persevere in the power of the Holy Spirit and not my strength. Help me daily to hold fast to my profession of Faith without wavering. In Jesus name, amen.

Gloria Strauthers

Write Your Plan
Make It clear
Pray Over It

Your Purpose Is Intentional

And the Lord answered me, and said, Write the vision, and make it plain upon tables, that he may run that readeth it.

Habakkuk 2:2 KJV

In life, we find ourselves as adults trying to figure out what it is that we are supposed to be doing or dedicating our time towards. We are in search of our calling or life mission as some may say. We are told all of our lives to enjoy being young, capitalize on your youth, and to focus on just being a kid in those moments. Then suddenly, you are a 17 or 18-year-old high school graduate in a completely new world, where your life is the direct example of your previous decisions.

It's okay to goal set and make a direct plan for your life. Vision boards and goal setting help paint the picture of your hearts desires and future goals to remind you of your focus.

It is critical to be intentional with your living. God left us a road map to write the vision, and make it plain so that we can see the vison and plan for our lives more clearly. Sometimes it matches God's will for our lives and sometimes He has something much bigger ahead! It's okay to speak positivity over your life, to control your mental thoughts, and to plan for your future.

If life has taught me anything, it has taught me to be "Intentional" in everything I do.

Challenge yourself to write out an outline and /or goal sheets for your personal and professional life. Write your plan, make it clear, and pray over it. I will not waste my time any longer crying over things of the past. I will no longer allow my past to control my future. I will no longer just allow life to just happen. I will be intentional in my prayers, intentional in my decisions, intentional in my daily walk. Challenge yourself daily to fight negative emotions, to speak positivity over your life, to stick to your vision and goals by speaking positivity over your dreams and visions and trusting God to bring them to fruition.

Prayer:

Father, I will be intentional on the things, people, and places in my life. I will trust God's plan and will for my life and I will put in the work. I'm blessed, highly favored, and intentional in my daily walk. I will have the life I intend on having, I thank God in advance. In Jesus mighty name, amen.

Jelisa Cook

Stir The Gift

Therefore I remind you to stir up the gift of God which is in you through the laying on of my hands. 7) For God has not given us a spirit of fear, but of power and of love and of a sound mind.

2 Timothy 1:6-7 KJV

Are you focusing on your talents or your gifts? We've become accustomed to the daily routines that society says we should as wives, moms & just being a woman. We've become good at our jobs, duties and skills; these are talents. Talent can be gained through training and sometimes are distractions from our gifts.

Gifts are the result of the power of God. Is your gift lying dormant? There is something in you that you know is supernatural, assigned to you from God. You may have put it aside so that you may focus on what the world views as success. You've become busy with growing the talents so that you can receive many accolades from the world, but there is a void. The time has come to stir your God given gifts. For it is only through your gifts that you are truly fulfilled and whole.

I was a teenaged mom, determined to create a "good" life for my children. By the age of 29, I had 3 children, a fiancée and was making what society calls "great money" I thought I was where I was supposed to be and doing what I was supposed to be doing. I was wrong.

From a child I had the gift of truly reaching people, encouraging them to see their own greatness, though I was not growing my own. By focusing on the talents, I had learned in my career, I had neglected the gift God implanted in me to encourage and empower others. This was my life until the feeling of emptiness became too much. Those around me couldn't understand why I would be unhappy, I couldn't explain it.

At 43 years old, while up late one night, I sat on the couch and asked, "Is this all for me?" I love my husband, adore my children but I needed to feel more than the titles of these duties. While sitting there, meditating on my question, I was reminded of how I had the desire, a calling, to help people, to elevate them and their thoughts.

I am a vessel.

Today I am an Integrative Health Coach and Speaker. I feel the Spirit when I speak to others about how it is never too late to achieve goals. This feeling within me is how I know this is my gift.

Your gifts are bigger than you and larger than the talents you have invested so much time in. When activating your gifts, you are being obedient and pleasing to God. You are unique, therefore so is your purpose. We need your gifts. Someone is waiting for you to walk in your purpose.

Will you stir your gift? Activate what God has placed in you so that you may walk fulfilled and excited about life again. Feel the joy that can only be felt when aligned with the Divine.

Trust God with no fear and step out on His promises. Live life how you are called to live.

Prayer:

Father, I come before You today to thank You for the gifts You have instilled in me. For You have blessed me from my mother's womb to be a light that You may shine to others. I asked that You forgive me for not investing more time with You to learn and grow what You have given me. May I have the knowledge and the courage to exalt You through my gifts, now and forever. In Jesus' name I pray, amen.

Nakia Morgan

Stop waiting on someone to validate your purpose. Own it and walk in it.

Girl You Got This

Press towards the mark of the high calling of GOD in Christ Jesus

Philippians 3:14

Girl you got this! You have gifts inside of you and someone somewhere needs your gifts. The gifts inside of you is a lifeline for someone, just like you. Your gift is needed. Know that God wants to use what He created and that means you.

Growing up I use to be very timid and shy. I called it being humble. Years ago, I was asked to be the mistress of ceremony of a women's event. I happen to be just five minutes late getting to the event that day. I was so timid and shy that I would not take the platform as the mistress of ceremoney. I told myself that the person filling in for me has a more powerful word than what I had. I called it being humble. How many know that's not God's will for my life or yours? God created each one of us with our very own special gifts and He wants to use us with the purpose of building His kingdom.

Yes! God gets all the Glory, so don't be afraid to go forth in the things that you are gifted and talented in. Your very gift will make room for you to prosper. A man's gift maketh room for him, and bringeth him before great men. (Pro 18:16). Your gift maybe the life source that will save some one's life. Never allow the enemy to tell you anything concerning your life. Remember he is the author of lies and there is no truth in him. Girl you got this; be encouraged. David encouraged himself in the Lord (1 Samuel 30:6)

Stop waiting for someone to validate you. (John 15:16) You are chosen and appointed by God. God validated you before you were born. You were validated in the womb. "Before you were born, I chose you to speak for me to the nations." (Jeremiah 1:5) Go forth in God and bear fruit-fruit that will last. Have faith that whatever you ask the Father in His name He will give you. (Deu 28:2)

Never let fear of any kind make you shrink back. You have gifts inside of you. The enemy's job is to keep you in fear and he goes to great lengths to keep you from walking in your gifts. We know that fear is from the enemy and God did not give us the spirit of fear. For God has not given us a spirit of fear, but of power and of love and of a sound mind. (2 Tim 1:7) You are fearfully and wonderfully made; Marvelous are the works of God's hands. (Ps. 139,14)

Maybe you are saying, "I don't know what my gift is?" My advice to you is to ask God to reveal to you your gifts. Once your gift is revealed to you, write them down and pray over them daily. Sometimes we have to inspire ourselves by going the extra mile. This means pressing in prayer, in praise, sometimes fasting and speaking our daily confessions over our lives into the atmosphere. This is how you fight a battle against forces of darkness that try to weight you down.

You must believe that God wants to use you and press in you win. It's your time to shine. Girl you got this! The price is far too high to let the gift inside of you be dormant. Girl you got this! Someone somewhere needs the gifts inside of you and is fighting to live.

Prayer:

Father thank You for all that you do in my life. I ask that You give me wisdom to use my gifts wisely to inspire and encourage others. Help me to look to You always so that I will be worthy of the gifts that You have placed on my life. Help me to press towards the mark of the high calling that You have placed on my life, that men will see Your great works and glorify YOU. In Jesus name, I pray, amen!

Debbie Cook

Doing it your way will not get you lasting results. You must consult the Father on instructions.

Surrender It All

Commit your actions to the Lord, and your plans will succeed

Proverbs 16:3 NLT

There are many times in our lives where we have these great plans according to what we believe our purpose is or in an effort to discover our purpose. The plans are good but they are not God. The plans are well thought out and make a lot of sense. We even run them by people whose opinion we trust and they are more excited than we are, so certainly we cannot be wrong.

As we attempt to follow those plans through, they don't turn out the way we thought or maybe it fails and we are left wondering why. We are confused as to why these great plans were not as successful as we envisioned it. How could they have not worked? I did everything right, but I didn't consult God on it. I didn't ask the creator of my purpose what was His will concerning my great plans.

We often assume that since the plans were a good thing that it was automatically a God thing. What if God wanted a date change because the people He wanted there were only available on that date but we chose the date that fit our schedule. Let us slow down and give God all of us so that we don't' miss the mark.

Prayer:

Father forgive me for all the times I did it my way and didn't consult You. Please forgive me for all the times I ignored Your instructions and still did it my way. Today I make a declaration that I will no longer do anything without running it by You first. I will no longer go with convenience or what seems easiest. I will commit all my actions to You so that my plans can succeed. In Jesus name, amen!

Chantea M. Willams

We Are Better Together

Form your purpose by asking for counsel, then carry it out using all the help you can get.

Proverbs 20:18 MSG

We must seek God consistently and diligently in order to know His perfect will for our lives. If we don't, we will find ourselves moving aimlessly through life only to one day look up and realize that we have not gone anywhere. Moses and the children of Israel wandered for forty years in the wilderness because of disobedience, fear, anger and disgust. God continued to provide for them, kept them, protected and nourished them. However, some of them did not make it to see the original promise, God still carried out His plan in the end and He will do the same thing for us.

To ensure that you achieve His promise for your life, follow His instructions completely and keep moving no matter what comes your way. His word says that He will never leave or forsake us and that He knows what is best for us. I encourage you to jump in with both feet, fear and all, to discover what God wants for your life and let His Word and His Spirit lead and guide you to fulfill your destiny. We must live our lives so that when we think about what we've done, we have no regrets.

It is imperative that we seek God and then allow Him to lead us to the right people who can help us carry out His mission. We are not here alone. God designed us to work together. Too many times, we argue and fight amongst each other or turn our noses up at our sisters, but *We Are Better Together.* Though we must be very attentive to those that we share with, God will allow your path to cross with those who you need to seek assistance. Do NOT take these people for granted because divine connections are very important in moving you from one level to the next and from fear to accomplishments.

Even the disciples had to work together while carrying out the assignments that Jesus gave them. We as children of God are no different. We have to be willing vessels and have an open mind to receive His instructions. We cannot put God in a box because He is much bigger than that. Make sure you know what you are looking for specifically as well because you'll be able to ask the right questions immediately. God desires for you to live a prosperous and healthy life, but you must be willing to do (act on) what He says. We must follow His plan in order to see the outcome He desires. Nothing is so important that we neglect to ask God what He wants before we move. STOP now and seek God for His instruction. Remember that *We Are Better Together!*

Are you ready to carry out His purpose?

Great, pray this prayer with me:

Prayer:

God, I come to you now, thanking you for another opportunity to get it right. I ask first that you forgive me for trying to do things the way I wanted without even considering your feelings or plans. You are so good that you allow me free will to do what I want and then come back to you seeking forgiveness when it doesn't work out. I know that you didn't have to forgive me Lord but I'm so thankful that you did. I declare that I will seek your counsel daily, listen to your instructions for my life and carry out your plan while seeking the help that I need. I will hear what people say, but I always come back to you for confirmation because my desire is to please you and you alone. It may not be easy, but it will definitely be worth it. I know that you didn't give me a spirit of fear but of love and of a sound mind so I will no longer be afraid when it comes to carrying out your will. In the matchless name of our Lord and Savior Jesus Christ I pray, Amen

Ronda Braden

When you understand your purpose clearly, you will start showing up in a more confident way.

A Heartful Purpose

The purposes of a person's heart are deep waters, but one who has insights draws them out.

Proverbs 20:5 NIV

Have you ever found yourself with a pen and notebook always in your hand? Or perhaps you spend hours in the kitchen preparing gourmet meals because it was what you like to do? Do you enjoy sewing or making craft items? Have you ever wondered if your talents or hobbies could be a part of your purpose?

Often our purpose is connected to our talents and hobbies. It is what you find yourself doing or daydreaming about a lot. As for me, I discovered my purpose when I was a teenager. I began writing poetry with a group of teenagers from my high school in our local newspaper. However, immediately, after graduating from high school, I no longer found time to write poetry. I was busy writing essays for my college classes. I was doing what I loved to do using my writing skills in a new way. As time went on and I moved into my career, I no longer had time to sit and write what I enjoyed doing the most.

My life became consumed with working full time in my career, raising my daughter, and being a wife. It was difficult juggling all my new tasks. There seem to be little time to slow down or even find a corner I could write quietly. I was living life but not fulfilling my purpose.

A few months before my 40th Birthday, I ask God to rekindle my purpose. I knew I enjoyed encouraging people through writing. God answered my prayers on June 14, 2018. I wrote my first book *Walking in God's Destiny*. I totally had to trust and lean on God through the process. My purpose was re-birthed, as I was encouraging others through writing again. The last two years, I have continued to write articles, speeches, affirmations, prayers and devotions. God has a purpose and plan for us all. We must seek Him and draw from His insight. He has equipped each one of us to fulfil that which He has called us too. Seek God and you will find your purpose. God will make a way for you to carry out your purpose.

Prayer:

Dear God, I think You for helping me to discover my purpose. I know You have a purpose and a plan for us all. If we just seek and ask You. You will reveal the plan unto us. I know You have given all of us talents and gifts to use for Your glory. Give us the wisdom, and insight to draw it out. Amen!

Keywana Wright

Do It Afraid

This is my command—be strong and courageous! Do not be afraid or discouraged. For the Lord your God is with you wherever you go.

Joshua 1: 9

One day, three powerful words were spoken over my life, and the whole game changed. DO IT AFRAID. Stifled by comfort, fear, self-doubt and all the "what-ifs" that I allowed my mind to travel to, I played it "safe" for years. What if I take that new job and it doesn't work out? What if I get this new mortgage, then can't afford to pay it? What if I start this new business and no one supports it? What if I end this friendship or relationship and have to be alone for a while?

That feeling of uncertainty, fear, and the human need to always have the answer to every question before moving forward often blocks us from the blessing that takes place on the other side of discomfort. The very thing that makes you afraid or gives you butterflies at the pit of your stomach, is calling you to a decision of choosing faith or fear. Choose faith, and do it afraid. What does this mean? It means that we have to trust that God is with us every step of the way. He blesses us for taking a leap of faith. He will bless our sacrifice. It does not mean that we won't still find ourselves grappling with the uncertainty, it means that we will boldly face the uncertainty knowing that God is within us.

That job that you want, take it. That business idea that you have, start it. That move to another state that you've always talked about, pack your bags. We are all being called into a season of crazy faith. A season of faith over fear. Everyone gets the call in their own way, but not everyone is strong and courageous enough to answer. A God-given talent, dream or idea wouldn't be placed inside of you, if you weren't already equipped with every single thing that you need to make it happen. The time is now. Your time is now. Be fearless, Queen.

Prayer:

Father, I thank You for being with me wherever I go. Father I thank You for the courageous spirit that you have given me. Father, in the moments when I let the spirit of fear enter my mind, help me to remember that You have not given us a spirit of fear, but of power and of love and of a sound mind. Father I thank You for the gifts that You have given me. Today I commit to developing my gifts, to using my gifts, to being fearless in all of my pursuits. God, I thank You. In Jesus name, Amen!

Stephanie Sherer

Best of Both Worlds, His Strength

My health may fail, and my spirit may grow weak, but God remains the strength of my heart; he is mine forever.

Psalm 73:26 NLT

I cannot imagine how different of a person I would be today had I only experienced growing up and living in one location.

In my opinion, I had the best of both worlds. In Mississippi I watched and participated in popping peas on the porch with my grandparents, making real homemade ice cream, while hearing the honking of cars as they drove by saying hey.

My California upbringing, I had to learn to take care of self, to separate feelings from business and to put things in writing with dates and signatures. To be okay with others not liking me. The focus was to make your own money with or without formal training or a degree.

To truly understand diversity and inclusion we must look beyond race, religion, sexual orientation, political status, zip codes, and our past disappointments. I want to encourage you to not allow your current zip code to be the only one you know throughout your entire life.

There's so much more out here in this world for us. Why settle? This is the time to think BIGGER. Don't you know we serve a God who created you and he has no limits?

Take the flight, book the cruise, move somewhere different, or start your own business. You will never know what you can achieve without taking the first step. Things will never be perfect, so the time is now. Step in Faith and hone into your own skills and resources.

When we pray for something God answers our prayers and provides us the strength to achieve them. Growing up one valuable lesson my mother taught her children was to explore, belong, and to travel. I would like to encourage you to read that line again and listen to the words carefully explore, belong and travel.

Explore the possibilities of the world. Experience different foods, cultures and careers. Belong where you go and walk into any room with confidence, OWN IT! Never leave your confidence or faith behind. Stop telling yourself it is too expensive and you cannot afford something. God's resources and funds are limitless.

Being different requires separations and will power. Use the strength of your own heart to be create your healthiest life and expand your horizon.

Put on your seatbelts and watch God lead you. Don't be afraid of failure or success. Continue stepping forward, and know He has you. You deserve it all.

Prayer:

Jehovah God, we come to You giving thanks. Thank You for the many options in this world. For all that You have created that allows us the opportunity to expand our wings. For the solo flights through storms and obstacles where we were uncertain. The lonely nights when the money was not enough to cover our expensive. Yet You allowed us to remain afloat. We give You the honor for we know our strength to continue this journey is only provided through You. We know that You have never left us. It is us who leaves You. Our marathon continues. In Jesus name, amen!

Tameka Garett

You have to be willing to walk in your purpose in order to enjoy the benefits of it.

Change Your Regimen

For I am about to do something new. See, I have already begun! Do you not see it? I will make a pathway through the wilderness. I will create rivers in the dry wasteland.

Isaiah 43:19 NLT

How are you feeling today? Oftentimes we hear that question as a patient visiting a doctor's office or about to go through some type of therapy. What if that were a question you asked yourself daily? As women we are born multi-taskers taking on the compiling duties as mother, wife, business/career professional, entrepreneur, homemaker, etc. and we keep running with one or a few of these roles until we sometimes experience mental and physical burnout. It's also possible to experience a spiritual drought due to the "overwhelming" duties or the combination of a few which can alter our daily intake of our spiritual regimen.

As women we keep up the juggling act but we never stop to ask ourselves the question, "How are you feeling today?" When was the last time you performed a check-up on your mental, physical and spiritual self? How would you rate it if you did? We don't realize how every component of our emotional being, our health and our time with God prepares us for our something new. How will you feel, act, or accept the new if you don't find out how you're doing or where you're heading as it relates to your God given purpose? Are you showing up on the healthy radar with a good diagnosis of your purpose or have you lost your daily regimen due to the foible moments in your compiled overwhelming life?

As women, it's important to have a daily regimen, almost like taking a daily vitamin. If you start today, you'll realize God desires to do something new in you. Take personal accountability and check yourself before you wreck yourself! You deserve it. Your purpose deserves it! You might not see results today by taking initiative to balance your compiled life but do it anyway.

Your future is healthy, blessed, thriving and full of endless possibilities of what you can become or accomplish. You will never reach purpose if you don't take a daily course of action. It's a big adjustment but you can do it! Be intentional, forgive yourself for your lack of self-care and create a regimen filled with ambition, dreams, goals and ideas. It's time to begin your day by looking in a mirror and asking yourself, "How are you feeling today?"

Father, forgive me if I've lost focus of my purpose. I believe everything will change as I change my regimen. In Jesus name, amen.

Tanya Randall

Persevere on Purpose

For I know the thoughts I think toward you, says the Lord, thoughts of peace and not of evil, to give you a future and a hope.

Jeremiah 29: 11 NKJV

Many times, in our lives, we often experience difficult challenges, some may appear to be impossible to deal with, undeserved circumstances, delayed promises, unanswered prayers and the list goes on. Which ultimately has left many women wounded, stagnant, depress and opening the door to rejection. However, I want to remind you the challenges your facing today has come to equip you for the woman you are becoming and to assure you that it's going to work out for the good!

According to Merriam website, the definition of persevere is *to persist in a state, enterprise, or undertaking in spite of counter influences, opposition, or discouragement.* Although you may be facing adversity, it's imperative that you are steadfast and unmovable. By this time, I'm sure you may be exhausted with trying things your way. You must solely depend on God. If He said it, then it seals the deal!

I dare you to trust God, let go of fear and step out on faith. Stop allowing your past to affect you negatively because you will cause more damage and only further delay your process. I'm not telling you something I didn't experience myself. I was once broken and bitter because of the tragic trauma in my life. The spirit of rejection had a grip on me. Alone and afraid, I begin to internalize the pain daily. I had been sexually violated, teenage mom, kidnapped, abused, almost homeless, a single parent and much more. Deep down in my heart I believe there was more to my life than what has happened to me.

My perspective on my life drastically shifted concerning what I've been through! I began to seek God and earnestly pray for direction and clarity. I begin to declare the Word of God over my life. I realize that I was not a victim or some sad charity case. I too, was more than a conqueror! What I had been through prepared me to help other women. Listen, God did it for me and He will do it for you! Out of the pain I once encountered and endured I gave birth to a phenomenal organization called *Her Story*.

I successfully excelled and graduated from Paul Mitchell Cosmetology School and shortly after became the owner of Salon Royalty, LLC. I was honored in *EntreprenHer Magazine*, as one of the top 50 inspirational speakers in the country! I became a published author, and currently obtaining my Master of Theology. To God be the glory and this is only the beginning. I say all that to tell you, now is the time to get your power back! Yes, that last blow hurt and knocked you down BUT get up! You've been there long enough, take dominion over every obstacle that was sent to destroy you and use it for The glory of God.

Ask yourself what is my assignment here on earth?

I have learned it's an awful thing to have exposure to sight but no vision. Having sight is just the ability to physically see what is in the natural realm; however, we walk by faith and not by sight. Vision requires an individual to think beyond their current circumstances. It causes barriers to be broken because there are no limitations. Self-development, discipline and strategic planning are necessary when pursuing your purpose. You may need to separate yourself for a while so that you can focus on you and your vision. Set aside special prayer time so you can hear God and He also lead you to a specific person to mentor you.

Prayer:

Father God in the name of Jesus, I asked that You would first forgive me of all my sins. Lord I asked that You heal and deliver me from every thing that goes against Your plans and purpose for my life here on earth. Create in me a clean heart and renew the right spirit within me. Father, I asked that You would transform my mind from into the mind of Christ. As of this moment, I have made a decision to overcome all doubt, negativity, fear, and procrastination. I am more then enough and I was created for a purpose, to serve others and bring glory to the Father. God I asked that You guild me in the way I should go and stir up the gifts that You have placed on the inside of me. Amen!

Georgette Cunningham

If you don't know who you are, then it will be more challenging to discover your purpose.

Me Finding Me

To Everything there is a season, and a time for every matter or purpose under heaven.

Ecclesiaste 3:1 AMPC

My entire world shifted and went upside down not too long ago. My life changed in ways that I had never imagined. See, I lost my beloved suddenly and unexpectedly. You can't plan for loss or wrap your head around something that would rock your world so deeply like this. How can you deal with the pain and anguish of a loss so deep that it literally changed who you are and the being in which you lived?

The path to healing leads me through many phases as I strived to let go of my grief. I found that having a support system, choosing to do self-care, picking up old hobbies that I once enjoyed and choosing to begin to enjoy life again made a tremendous impact. The impact allowed me to begin to peel back the layers that I was holding on to and to discover me again who once was outgoing, fun-loving and happy. This by far was not overnight. This transformation took a lot of hard work and discipline to reach my goal of being the old me. Prayers, church attendance, therapy, journaling, and learning to let go and not feel guilty is what helped me.

This event happened almost three years ago, and I can sometimes replay it in my head just like it happened yesterday. I can remember what I had on, the smells, the visions, and the sounds. This loss leads me to who I am today. A best-selling author in the US and internationally, certified Grief Coach, and the founder of The Healing Group Community, LLC. The titles that I now hold have become purpose for me and give me great pleasure. I am so elated to be able to be in this space. What if this loss hadn't happened, would I be in this same space? Would my life's work in this season be to still help others let go of pain and grief while helping to find positive actions after a loss? We are given a gift from the Father Almighty and it is our mission to work to achieve the purpose that was set before we were in our Mother's womb.

How do we know what our mission and purpose are in life? We have to study the Word of God to find out what he wants us to do. We are equipped to be great and Our Father is the one who is waiting on us to fulfill what he has placed in us to help others. We are destined to carry out and fulfill the purpose we have in our life. The call that is on our lives is one of greatness, attainment and truly, our direction.

Prayer:

Most matchless and loving Father, let me walk in my purpose and learn to accept what You have placed in me. Let me not be afraid to accept that I am supposed to do in my life in order to help others. Prepare me to carry out your will and to be a helper of all helpers in the areas where I should be. Allow me to accept what Your perfect will is for my life and let me carry out the plan in which You have sanctioned just for me. May I be able to see the purpose in my life as I help others let the pain go! In Jesus almighty name I pray, amen!

Cherie Barnes

As you walk in your purpose, you will become more confident in yourself.

Transformed Wholeness in God

And the very God of peace sanctify you wholly; and I pray God your whole spirit and soul and body be preserved blameless to the coming of our Lord Jesus Christ

1 Thessalonians 5:23-24 KJV

I was looking in all the wrong places for what I needed to make me whole. No clear direction and purpose. Feeling like I was bleeding and trying to find something, a band-aid to cover my hurt. Looking at other people to try and make me feel whole. Being co-dependent in relationships. Seeking others out to heal the hurts. Sometimes even acting in ways that were harmful. Trying to achieve, seeking my purpose, my fullness, my wholeness in my strength and abilities, yet it never yielded the best outcomes in that season. When I sought others and things to make me whole, I wound up broken, confused and lacking. I did not see my purpose. My soul hurt and yearned for that which I did not know, and within myself I screamed loudly, but those around me heard me not.

Eventually, the realization hit that if I wanted to find my purpose, true wholeness, then transformation must come forth through God's leading; in alignment with biblical truth, using Jesus as the example. If wholeness is what we desire, then we must invite God into the deepest part of whom we are. We must invite Him into our spirit and ask Him to transform us from the inside out, so we can begin to see our purpose clearly.

I didn't know it, but I was like so many people, hurting from the blows that life had dealt me. Learning how to function in the midst of my mess and pain. All the while not knowing that Jesus loved me beyond my foolishness.

Once I accepted the Lord as my Savior, change began to gradually take place in my life for the better. Daily I began to grow in my relationship with Christ. Then He began to reveal the depth of my brokenness to me.

Scripture declares, "And the very God of peace sanctify you wholly; and I pray God your whole spirit and soul and body be preserved blameless to the coming of our Lord Jesus Christ" (1 Thessalonians 5:23-24).

In the biblical context, the Lord wants us to be holistically well. He wants our mind, body, spirit to be in alignment with Him. Thus, when any aspect of our being is not well, the other elements are adversely and significantly affected. We must know that when a person is whole, there can still be struggles, pains, and other life issues to arise. The wholeness is in Christ, not what is going on. Wholeness is having the Lord's joy, even when things are not going the way we anticipate in our life. Wholeness is not contingent on one's life situations and circumstances.

Each person can conform within their discomfort that leads to their wholeness. Each person's environment and life experiences significantly contribute to their personality. The challenge is to ask and allow the Holy Spirit to transform us; into His predestined plan for our life. Having a submission daily to the Lord will help us depend on Him for all our needs and direction. As we submit, we allow ourselves guidance by principles found in the bible – the resulting outcome is in alignment with how God designed His plan for our lives. As Paul said in the scripture above, our wholeness comes only through God.

Prayer:

Father of Glory You have been so great to me. I thank and praise You for all that You are and do for me. I thank You for guiding me on this journey of wholeness through Your transforming power. If my heart is troubled, remind me that I am whole in You. If my strength starts to fail, remind me that I am complete in You. If my arms become weak from carrying a load that is too heavy, remind me to give it to You. May I stay focused and committed in Your truth so that I will be on the right path that leads to positive and productive outcomes. That my wholeness may be complete in You. Please, help me to keep my mind focused on you. Please, give me the needed courage, faith, and perseverance to allow You to lead. I glorify and praise Your Holy and Righteous name, amen!

Dr. Annette West

Don't allow the challenges in your life to stop you from living in your purpose. Use it as a motivation to keep going.

Love From the Inside Out

For no man yet hateth his own flesh; but nourisheth and cherisheth it, even as the Lord the church.

Ephesians 5:29 KJV

Growing up in most Christian churches there is no denial all know the two greatest commandments. We must love the Lord your God with all your soul, mind, and your strength and to love your neighbor as you love yourself. We are taught that to deny ourselves is the first evidential proof that we are modeling ourselves after the unfailing love of Jesus Christ. This perpetual act of loving and serving others while putting the needs of others above our own is often a great reflection of Christ's love toward us.

The silent clause that is often left undiscussed is that in the scripture is, "Love others as you would love yourself." That is impossible to love someone effectively if you do not know how to first love yourself. The mystery and confusion surfaces when you compare the two narratives of denying oneself but also loving others as you would love yourself.

So how do we deny ourselves but think that it's wrong to deny others? What exactly would need to be denied? Access, overuse, and the need to say yes or the need to please everyone. The need to please others and the inability to say no is a trait that is most often identified in Christians who have completely denied themselves thus resulting in many not knowing how to set boundaries or feeling an emotional conviction for doing so.

We cannot love others effectively if we do not first practice self-love, self-awareness and the establishment of much needed boundaries. We cannot assist with emotional, spiritual, or physical healing for others if we do not take the time to attend to our own wellbeing and wholeness. In 3 John 1:2 it states, "I wish above all that you may prosper and be in health even as our soul prospers." John is expressing his desire for us to be whole and have balance both spiritually and naturally. We must learn that self-love does not in no wise reflect selfishness or mean that one loves themselves above others but that one is aware enough to be aware of the need to tend to your own wounds, take time to refuel and have your spirit replenished.

There is a saying "you teach people how to treat you". I believe this is so true, but we must not teach them simply in word but also in deed. While we are building a life to serve let's build a life worth living. Love yourself right so that others can do the same. Lets all practice love-from the inside out.

Prayer:

Dear God,

Thank You for being my everything. Thank You for Your love towards me. Today I realize that I may have loved unbounded. I may have not considered the love for my self as important. Teach me to love myself as You love me. Teach me to forgive myself as You forgive me. Teach me to value myself as You value me. As I love others, please help me to know my limit and when I should set myself aside to practice self-care. I realize that I am of no value to others if I'm not whole, if my cup has not been refilled, and if I do not set boundaries. I love that You love me and I will be faithful in the area of loving myself. My grateful will forever continue to flow and my love for others will always extend beyond personal self-gain. Thank You for teaching me boundaries and showing me my true value in Your eyes. In Jesus name, amen!

Javion Woods-Jamess

Trouble does not last always! Keep moving forward!

Put Doubt Out

But when the crowd was put outside, He went in and took her by the hand, and the girl arose.

Matthew 9:25 KJV

During the Fall season after my 40th birthday, I attended my first mammogram. The appointment was brief, and simple, but for some reason was a little awkward. On the day after the appointment, I received a phone call from my doctor with information that a nodule was detected in the right breast and that I would be scheduled for a follow-up in 2 weeks.

One would have to admit that I was concerned, and the 'what-if's began to play over and over in my head. What if, I am sick? What if, it is cancer? Then the prayer, "Dear God, please don't let it be cancer!" Realizing that negative thoughts were trying to overwhelm, that is when I reached out to a Mother in my church. Upon talking to her, she suggested reading the New Testament and meditating on scriptures where Jesus healed the sick and afflicted. Taking her advice, joy was found and rejuvenation. I soon realized that throughout the Gospels, Jesus healed many people, which encouraged me, and I thought, "Wow! Jesus healed everyone who believed!"

Two weeks later, when during my second mammogram screening, was when I came to the conclusion that whatever the outcome of this appointment, God is with me! There is nothing impossible for Him not even cancer. Unlike the first appointment, this one was not simple or brief. After being called into the X-ray room three times, and having the radiologist called in, the doctor performed the ultrasound. Finally, the doctor advised the nodule seen in the first screening was no longer there. To say I was overwhelmed with joy is an understatement! All that could be uttered was, "Praise God, Jesus healed people back, then and has done it again. Why, because Hhe has personally done it for me."

This experience brought to mind Matthew 9 and the story of a ruler whose daughter died and he came to Jesus to ask Him to come to his house and raise his daughter to life. Jesus upon entering the ruler's house, found a crowd of mourners inside of the home- wailing for the girl. After Jesus rebuked the mourners and told them to leave, He said, "The girl isn't dead. She's only asleep." The crowd laughed, therefore, Jesus put the crowd out. Jesus then fulfilling the rulers request, laid hands on his daughter and she was brought back to life. Just as Jesus needed to put out those who didn't believe, we must do the same in our own lives. Our purpose is our identify and any unbelief must be put out, so that the girl that is inside of us can be raised.

Therefore, I want to encourage you to face any trial or difficulty with belief and faith in Jesus. He is always with us and we need only to ask God to come into our lives, and take control. There are situations only God can do, and in those moments doubt must be put out, so our whole heart can God. Remember, faith is believing even when it looks impossible. Where there is faith, doubt cannot stay. Doubt is pondering negatively on situations and circumstances that are contrary or different from what we are believing God for. We must not let anyone or anything cause us to doubt or give up. We must persevere through our emotions and trust God's plans for us. Some things God will answer immediately, some things we will see the answer manifested over time. Trust, believe God and put doubt out.

Prayer:

Heavenly Father, we thank You for Your presence. Help us to trust You for all thing, our healing , deliverance and life's purpose. Help us to walk by faith, and not by sight- no matter what comes our way. Bless the reader of this devotion by meeting their needs, and bless their desire to serve You. In Jesus' name, amen.

Louise Davis

Your purpose is tied to your faith.

In Times of Trouble Say...

Call upon Me in the day of trouble; I shall rescue you, and you will honor Me.

Psalm 50:15

Our purpose is dependent upon how we handle adversity. How our hearts respond to the troubles in this world has a severe effect on our purpose. What do we say when adversity comes? Does our conversation match the faith spoken of in the Word of God? Or better yet, does it reflect the God revealed in the scriptures or the one we have "boxed in" in our thoughts? Although, it's the last thing anyone wants, it is unavoidable. It is impossible to be God's child and not encounter them.

As, we live, breathe, move through this earth, each of us will have some form of trouble. It may occur in our finances, health, family, places of employment. However, either way, there is a purpose, a divine reason God has allowed it to filter through His fingers of love... whether we understand the reason or not. No matter what it is, we must not allow it to push us away but draw us closer to Him.

I deal with various autoimmune disorders, but there is one that could disrupt my life if I choose to allow it – Fibromyalgia. When I was first diagnosed, I had zeal to conquer it in my own strength and attempted to pray it away. By the time year four came, I was worn out and all but given up. During this period, I was not living out my purpose. I focused on how much pain I was in and did not seek God. This caused my heart and mind to become toxic. I had become infectious.

We choose who or what to focus on. The more we focus on the problem, the weaker we become. We lose our strength. Distraction becomes our current state of mind and that which we are purposed to do will either be delayed or unfulfilled. However, if we give them over to Him, He clears our minds and our perspective changes. We are filled with His light and renewed. Our callings not only become crystal clear, but there is a new energy with which to fill them.

He does not promise to remove challenges, situations, or disappointments. These should draw us closer to Him. The One who has given your life meaning, is the One we are to run to when the way seems dark and the obstacles are insurmountable. He is the way of escape provided, our refuge which is found when we call upon Him. Total submission to Him, reveals complete faith in His timing and method of rescue. This faith is the bridge from knowing what is said about God to standing on who we believe Him to be by faith without conditions. Purpose depends on how we react during troubled times. We must know what we believe in times of trouble so we will know what to say when it comes.

In time of trouble, say, "First, He brought me here; it is by His will I am in this strait place; in that fact I will rest." Next, "He will keep me here in His love, and give me grace to behave as His child." Then say, "He will make the trial a blessing, teaching me the lessons He intends me to learn, and working in me the grace He means to bestow. And last, "In His good time He can bring me out again – how and when, He knows." Therefore, say "I am here, (1) By God's appointment, (2) in His keeping, (3) under his training, (4) for His time." - **Andrew Murray**

Prayer:

Majestic and Sovereign God, I thank You for every situation You've allowed me to go through. Forgive me for not focusing on You and Your divine will. Bring to the surface every fear that troubles and torments me. Replace them with Your liberating love. Give me the strength to become settled with who You are in Your Word so that I may not only stand firm but also speak boldly with confidence in and of You. For, how I handle trials will determine how successful I am in carrying out your will for my life. In Jesus name, amen!

LaQuetia Gilliard

When God has you on a temporarily pause, don't take it as a rejection. It's for your protection.

A Life With Grace and Mercy

Trust in the Lord with all thine heart; and lean not unto thine own understanding. In all thy ways acknowledge him, and he shall direct thy paths.

Proverbs 3:5-6 KJV

Over the years my life journey has been through many stumbling blocks, dark and bumpy roads, and rocky mountains. I can go on and on. I am sure that you can relate to some of the same situations and challenges through your life journey. I once felt that I always made the wrong choices, decisions, friends and jobs. I wanted only to discover my hopes, dreams and desires that God had for me and it was very challenging with many hurts, pains and tears along the way.

During this time, I prayed to God all the time about all the "wrong" things that was happening to me. I would always ask God to forgive me for wrong thinking, wrong thoughts, and wrong words about myself. I will never forget the first time I heard The Mississippi Mass Choir singing the song *Your Grace and Mercy* as I was driving to a job interview. I had to pull over so I could focus on the words of the song. It was as though they were singing to me. I'm living this moment because of God's grace and mercy.

Have you ever experienced a feeling like that? Think about it. I pulled myself together and continued to my interview, which was an organization that provided services for people with developmental disabilities. I never worked with people with disabilities before and I didn't have the education; even though I have always had a passion for anyone with a disability in the community. I was offered the position as a coordinator for one of the programs. I thought I had made another wrong choice. The more I learned about God's grace and mercy, the more my life became a faithful transformation of His glory.

What was so amazing? Within a year, the employability program for individuals with developmental disabilities became a model program not only for the local community, but for the county and statewide. This part of my life journey was not my desire, but it is God's choice of purpose for my life; to impact a focus in their communities on their abilities more than their disabilities. Wow! Isn't that amazing? I learned that things you really know how to do is a gift from God. When you are chosen to do something that you have no skills, ability or desire is God's purpose.

Regardless of the stumbling blocks, dark and bumpy roads and rocky mountains that you may continue to experience in life; just know that God is preparing you for a special assignment. You must believe that God's grace is a sufficiency of His unconditional love and His mercy endures forever. You must understand that the purpose you desire for yourself can be limited, but His purpose for you will be everlasting. You will be preoccupied with greater things because you are *fearfully and wonderfully created* as a key ingredient for God's purpose for your life. So, don't let your past, present or future make you feel like you have no purpose in life. God's grace and mercy will help you soar like an eagle with wings that you didn't know you had through your life journey. As John Henry Newman once stated, *"Do not fear that your life will come to end, but rather that it will never truly begin."* Remember the only impossible journey in life is the life you never really begin.

Prayer:

Father, I stretch my hands to Your forgiveness for not acknowledging Your grace and mercy during my life's journey. I thank You that You have a high purpose for my life. Please help me to know what that purpose is. I want to do great things for You, but I know that only You can make that happen for me. So, I surrender myself totally to You. Lord, I give You my life and want to be used for Your glory. I with trust in You, Lord with all your heart and will lean not on my own understanding. In all Your ways acknowledge Him and He will make my path straight. In Jesus name, Amen!

Sherrie Truelove

When God has you on a temporarily pause, don't take it as a rejection. It's for your protection.

In Between the Wait

But they that wait upon the Lord shall renew their strength; they shall mount up with wings as eagles; they shall run, and not be weary; and they shall walk, and not faint.

Isaiah 40:31 KJV

What does it mean to wait? I can only speak for myself and say that when I hear the word wait, it reminds me of standing in line at the tax office, grocery store, or the ladie's restroom after a theater production. To wait in the biblical context according to the Hebrew (which is qavah) means, "to bind together". Understand that "to bind together" does not mean for us to stand still or be seated quietly waiting on something to happen. It's means to commune with Him.

God wants to strengthen you as you wait. That's why you must open up your mouth and give Him praise *In Between the Wait.* Even when you don't understand what's going on, remember that God LOVES you. Allow yourself to see the beauty in the wait as you praise God. Be brave and courageous. Yes, wait patiently for the Lord.

Today, I speak life to your heaviness. Gird yourself up, trust God, and reset your focus. God is not mad at you. He's waiting on you to lay it all at his feet. Set the atmosphere with praise and worship God with your whole heart. Wait with such expectation, that it infects everyone you meet.

1) Only believe. (Mark 5:36 KJV) Believe that all things are possible. Believe to see God's manifested goodness.

2) Trust God through the process. (Proverbs 3:5-6 KJV)

3) Give thanks. (Psalms 107:1-2 NLT) Regardless of where you are right now, stir yourself up and with a loud voice speak of his goodness.

4) Rest (Matt 11:28-30 MSG) Take a minute to pause and reflect on the goodness of God. Selah

Prayer:

Lord give me the desire and patience to wait on You and not move in my own timing. In Jesus name, amen!

Irene Watson

The Other Side Of Pain

But they that wait upon the Lord shall renew their strength; they shall mount up with wings as eagles; they shall run, and not be weary; and they shall walk, and not faint.

Romans 8:28 NIV

Objects in the mirror are closer than they appear. This is the phrase, or some variation thereof, that is found on a vehicle's rear-view mirror. It is a reminder that we cannot take life experiences at face value. Mirrors serve as useful tools. They were not only created for self-examination, but also to bring attention to what (or who) is in our immediate background. However, there is danger in focusing on our reflection: The ugly scars of our past and our pain can appear magnified in our lives and prevent us from moving forward in our purpose. We fixate on our imperfections, failures, and scars or we feel unqualified because of our past and our pain.

Let's remember, the phrase that is imprinted on mirrors will also expose what is behind us as well. It can remind us of past hurts, but it can remind us of how we overcame. Superimposing the image, God layers Himself over our inadequacies and imperfections so that He becomes the focus. When discovering our purpose, we should examine our experiences through God's eyes. God can use our strengths and our weaknesses for His glory. He will use those attempts on the life of your destiny and those trials to reveal your purpose. The Word tells us that in all things God works for the good of them who love Him. Your past, your pain, and your purpose are all connected.

Living a life of heartache, brokenness, addiction, abuse, loss, or even abandonment can be debilitating. God can and will use it for edification and to break the chains of bondage in someone's life. The enemy seeks to create chaos in our lives by causing pain. But, beloved, there is power on the other side of pain. There is peace on the other side of pain. There is purpose on the other side of your pain. This power, this peace, and purpose is only found in Him. Your life-- your story--holds powerful purpose. When we open our heart to acknowledge our pain, our calling--our purpose is found. When we allow God to be glorified in our weakness, we can heal.

There is purpose just on the other side of your pain.

Lord forgive me for relying on my own strength and not allowing You to use my pain to discover my purpose in You. Thank You for loving me through my weakness and for working ALL things out for my good and for the good of others. In Jesus name, amen!

Jennifer Gray-Wymbs

Death Is Not The End

You have turned my mourning into joyful dancing. You have taken away my clothes of mourning and clothed me with joy, that I might sing praises to you and not be silent. O Lord my God, I will give you thanks forever!

Psalm 30: 11-12 NLT

The death of a love one, a best friend or a special someone leaves us in a space of disbelief. We get angry with God, we question Him, we question His motives and we even play the blame game with Him. My best friend and sister of 26 years left the physical world to be with the Lord two years ago. I went through an emotional and mental breakdown because my best friend, my sister and confidant was no longer here with me. I no longer had anyone to share my deepest feelings with, that one person who was non-judgmental, that one person that I could go to and pray and fast with when I felt like the world was beating up on me.

Two years before she gained her wings, she and I had talked about starting a business. We had no idea where to start but we knew this was our calling in life and we wanted to do something that encouraged others. We finally came up with the idea for making jewelry that had special meaning, biblical scriptures and so forth, but of course, that dream never happened. Fast-forward a year after she gained her wings, I made the decision to start the business we talked about together. In the beginning, I was excited and wanted to make her proud but the more I did the more I missed her. I had gotten to a point where I no longer wanted to be a part of the business world. I struggled for days, weeks and months to move forward without her. I felt that I was not capable of doing what God instructed me to do because I am not strong in His word and teachings like my best her. Then one day, I remembered my purpose to deliver plans of God to the people.

Through my trials, tribulations and the death of my sister I had to understand that giving up on life and my purpose was not an option. Then one day, I received a word from my sister through the Holy Spirit. She said, "Stop pining over me, because I am in a better place." That is when I remembered, Jesus tells us not to concern ourselves with believers who have physically left but we should look forward to His promise return as well as the return of those who have fallen asleep. Jesus desires that we support, love, and teach others about Him. Receiving salvation through Jesus Christ is how we can be reunited with our love ones.

I truly believe when you are in the presence of God at all times, all of your trials and tribulations are easier to deal with, including the death of our loved one. God is our greatest strength. God has said, "Never will I leave you; never will I forsake you."

Prayer:

Father God, thank You for your teachings and Your unwavering word. You have always shown me who You are through my blessings and my trials. Father, You have placed individuals in my life that has helped me in my journey of learning Your word so that I am able to share with others. Father, thank You for showing my sister and me our purpose and allowing me to move forward in it without her, I know she would be proud. Thank You for not giving up on me, Thank You for protecting me mentally, emotionally, physically and spiritually. Last but not least, thank You for allowing my best friend/sister and me to have an amazing 26 years. This I pray is in the name of our Lord and Savior Jesus Christ, amen.

Sharolyn Jackson-Douglas

Your Purpose Matters

The Purpose Walk

Be strong. Take courage. Don't be intimidated. Don't give them a second thought because God, your God, is striding ahead of you. He's right there with you. He won't let you down; he won't leave you.

Deuteronomy 31:6 MSG

Have you ever been discouraged during your walk with Jesus? Have you asked yourself why people become cold and forget how far Jesus has brought them? Life had beat me up with the suicide of my son, incarceration of my now ex-husband who has a life sentence, and incarceration of myself. I became so numb I was waking up every day non-intentional and unpurposed. I had to spend some real time with God because I found myself at rock bottom, with no foundation and spiritually dead. I had to amp up my time with Him, get honest with myself and realize I was hurt, heartbroken and only God could fix me.

The first year I was saved after years of being in The Nation of Islam, I had a tremendous zeal for God. I joined every auxiliary possible, attended a bunch of conferences, and bought a completely new church wardrobe, just to discover I was busy but nonproductive.

During my walk, my faith has been tested over and over again. See many think being a part of the Kingdom of God is enough. Work and action are necessary. I had to realize I was a victim of identity theft, because I had no clue who I was in Christ. An encounter with my Father reminded me of my original lineage. I was reminded of who I belonged to and the realization of why I am here on this Earth became clear. My purpose was revealed that I am a soldier who is to adapt and overcome.

God has used my mouth to encourage people who were suicidal or experienced the tragedy of having a loved one take their life. God hides His people in many places. I can testify to coming into the light after being bound up in religion.

Every one of us has a purpose and assignment to be completed before we leave this Earth. At times this walk gets challenging and persecution exists and will happen. We can find ourselves questioning God, which is challenging Him and demanding an answer. We can always ask Him a question but never question Him. Simply asking Him the question, "Father what is my purpose? What is your will for my life?" Trust He will answer you. He will guide and show us. He will order our footsteps, giving us visions, a mission, a purpose and provision to get it done. It takes us to step out on faith and trust that He is sovereign and sits on the throne. He is God yesterday, today and forevermore. Knowing your identity is key. You are the head not the tail. You are the lender not the borrower. You are an heir to the Kingdom. You are a Kingdom of God ambassador. You represent Him everywhere you go.

Your walk is different as you spend time with your Father. You become grounded and unmovable during the storms of life. Like trees in a hurricane, some sway but still stand. We are to stand and not be discouraged or dismayed. We will realize the storms are necessary for our walk. .

Our creator did not make a mistake when He created us. We are here for our fellow brothers and sisters and to advance God's Kingdom. It the how YOU should be doing it that we need to be clear on.

Prayer:

Father forgive me for even second guessing you. You are the ONLY living God and You don't renege on Your promises. Help us to remain on course and faithful to do the work of your kingdom. No matter what it looks like we know You are always victorious. I commit and submit to Your will for my life. For You are that Great I Am. In Jesus name, amen!

Antoinette Holman

You have to make a decision to go after what has already been given to you!

Queen Up

For we are God's masterpiece. He has created us anew in Christ Jesus, so we can do the good things he planned for us long ago.

Ephesians 2:10 NLT

Faith in God will elevate you to next level and perhaps someone else's faith in you. As a mother, I would affirm to my children through making sure they always knew how worthy they are. However, I took it a step further and I showed up to be the Queen I am. I understood the importance of the power of our actions and being the role model that our next generations needs to see.

Positive affirmations allow you to consciously activate and elevate principles such as love, selfless service, and next level mindsets. It allows you to become the Queen you are ordained to be. As my children continued to grow and develop, they walked into their destiny. They were creating milestones after milestones and accomplishments that help develop their interpersonal and leadership skills.

The Queen I am Knows:

(a) *Self-Improvement* is a must. The most important task of life is the person you become. Self-improvement is critical for human beings to evolve. It helps and individual understand their strengths and weakness. An important aspect of self-improvement is to make sure you are always improving in any area of your life, physically, mentally, emotionally, professionally, etc. This will always keep you in a queen status.

(b) *Total Belief in Oneself* is a must. Our mind is truly amazing when we believe in its power as a tool for manifesting our purpose and intention. There is nothing that can stop you. Queen Up Status! We are the creators of what we think and feel; if we can nourish a limiting thought or belief, then we can just as easily do the same for a non-limiting one. If we can build walls in our mind that obstruct our progress, then we can definitely knock them down. We are all gifted with the innate power to attract our deepest desires into our physical space — we only need to believe that we can! Total belief in oneself is what breaks generational curses and solve the many solutions that we are created to resolve.

(c) *The Importance of Healing.* When our bodies experience physical injuries, we don't hesitate to take necessary measures for healing. However, we should have the same concept for when we experience mental injuries from traumatic circumstances that can alter our way of life. What if your body never healed? What if you still had every scratch you have ever gotten? What if every bone you have ever broken stayed that way? Think of every bump, bruise, and burn. Every nick and cut. What would you look like if your body never healed? We would be a mess! That is what happens when we don't mentally heal from misfortunes of life. Queens, know you must heal from your situations. Seek help that will allow you to overcome, breakthrough, and heal. Don't try to hide or coverup the hurts. For me it was the process of facing and healing my inner child. To heal your inner child is to me the ultimate expression of self-love, and healing. To put it bluntly without which we are never going to become a truly whole and balanced person. Lay them open before God. Pour out your heart and soul. He will listen and as you hear his voice, he will guide you to healing. You will find that he is the ultimate healer.

Today we must "Queen Up" and know that this journey is not just about you but the legacy that you can impact. You are destined for major things and to solve many solutions in this world. As Queens we never compare, compete, nor complain. You have complete belief in you NO MATTER WHAT…She graces herself in scripture Psalm 139:14 NLT Thank you for making me so wonderfully complex! Your workmanship is marvelous—how well I know it. Your crown which is your integrity, the value you add to others, and the ability to always make next level movements, so "Queen UP"!!

Father God I come to as I must humbly know how, in thanksgiving and praise. Allow me to be convicted when I am not operating in my greatness and to consistently show up as royal representation of You. In Jesus name, amen!

Dr. Jennifer Boyer

God has already graced you to handle whatever He allows to come your way.

No More Hustling Just Chase After God

"Tell those rich in this world's wealth to quit being so full of themselves and so obsessed with money, which is here today and gone tomorrow. Tell them to go after God, who piles on all the riches we could ever manage—to do good, to be rich in helping others, to be extravagantly generous. If they do that, they'll build a treasury that will last, gaining life that is truly life."

1 Timothy 6:17-19 MSG

If we are all honest with ourselves, we will admit that starting a business can be overwhelmingly exciting, intimidating and quite scary at times. Whether you're new in business or past the startup phase, it is very easy to get caught up in worldly thinking when it comes to being rich. We are made to believe that you must hustle hard in order to get big. We are made to believe that money will solve all of our business problems. We even believe that being connected to the "right" people will get you in the right places.

How often as business owners, do we find ourselves focusing so much on the almighty dollar? How often are we dreaming about that rich life, reading post after post, skimming blog after blog, and downloading strategy after strategy to calculate your riches?

Here is what I've learned from being in business. Being connected to people is not always the right answer to your problems. Hustling hard will leave you isolated, broke and with less energy. You can have all the money in the world and not be happy.

The scripture says we are not to become obsessed (hustlers listen in) with being rich and "living that life".

Hustling is an obsessed mindset. This type of obsession can make us so selfish in our ways. We'll constantly think about what it takes for us to get to the next level. We'll constantly think about what WE can do accomplish more and that becomes our drive. This type of obsession brings about the need to have our lives in the limelight of others but not being a light to the world as Christ calls us to be. Seeking after riches and let's not forget possessions gives the world a false sense that riches and obsessions bring joy.

The Bible says seek first the kingdom AND all of His right ways. I learned these lessons the hard way after following the wrong advice and working so hard, countless hours of no sleep and family time that my home life was in disarray. Our God doesn't want us to have a lack in any area of our lives. He even commands us to rest. He wants us to live a life of abundance. He wants us as kingdom entrepreneurs to have impact and influence. However, we must understand that our wealth only comes through Him. We have to go after God, chasing and embracing His will AND THEN all will be added unto us, overflowing and much more.

Prayer:

Father we thank you for opportunities to expand our reach, increase our wealth, and impact the kingdom through entrepreneurship. Forgive us if we have not put you first as we know that you require us to draw closer to you. Bless our minds, our work and everyone we reach.

Tamika Shuler-Washington

Your Purpose Matters Affirmation:

The Lord will work out His plans for my life.

He will not abandon me.

He has already qualified and favoured me.

I will obey all His instructions so that I can enjoy all of His benefits.

He has made my purpose to matter for many.

It is all working together for my good to bring Him glory.

Meet the Authors

Cherie Barnes

Cherie is an Author, Speaker, Clinician and Certified Life & Grief Coach in the Greater Chicagoland Area. Cherie helps others in their grief journey by letting them know is okay to grieve and that you can overcome and be well in the journey. Cherie is the Principal & Owner of The Healing Group Community, LLC which is a consulting, counseling, coaching and mentoring company to help individuals with life transitions, grief & loss as well as trauma. Cherie has written and published 3 books about grief and loss and created a number of products both audio and digital surrounding grief topics and empowerment.

Dr. Jennifer Boyer

Jennifer Boyer is a renowned public speaker, author and dance minister. Dr. Jennifer Boyer has risen to prominence by delivering a high-energy speeches that motivate others to transform their lives in greatness. It is messages taken from her own life that is formed into powerful teaching moments. Dr. Boyer's straight-from-the-heart, passion and high-energy, motivates audiences to step beyond their limitations and into their greatness in many ways.

Dr. Boyer was born into poverty, and traumatizing situations that left her homeless at the age of 16. She birth two amazing children out of wedlock but broken generational cycles by empowering and denying the generational curses. With facing many stumbling blocks as a child, and young woman, Dr. Boyer knew she had to move into the culture of change as she continues to bring changes to many others. Dr. Boyer is committed to motivating and training today's generation to be achievers and leaders as she empowers others every day with Motivational Moments and speaks on many platforms to bring Transitional Transformation Mindsets.

Dr. Boyer truly believes in the power of formal education, self-education, and self- empowering. She recently received her Honorary Doctorate Degree in Leadership from Abundant Life Bible College and Theological Seminary. She is currently writing her first book, *Saving Our Families*. Formal education will make you a living; self-education will make you a fortune." "I cannot teach anybody anything, I can only make them think." "The only person who is educated is the one who has learned how to learn and change." Next Level Thinking!

Ronda Braden

R onda is the owner of R Braden Enterprises, which provides virtual assistant services to small business owners. She is an advocate for grandparents and their participation (interaction) in the lives of their grandchildren. It is because of an awesome relationship with her own grandmother that she feels so passionately about this.

Ronda aspires to one day have a nonprofit organization addressing this very important issue. Ronda has been Billing/Payroll Specialist for 20+ years with a medical staffing agency. She has also received her Associates Degree from St. Louis

Community College and is working towards obtaining her Bachelors' in Business Administration.

She is a mother of six and has five wonderfully awesome grand children with whom she loves to spend her free time.

Debbie Cook

As a #1 Best-selling and #1 New release of the "Treasures In My Heart the Journey of 12 Women" author Debbie Cook is known as the Love Doctor. Dee is a worshiper and lover of God who is a 2017 Graduate of Dr. Cindy Trimm's Kingdom School of Ministry.

Dee is also the founder of The Worship Room with Minister Dee, internet radio show "Your Hour of Power", a Certified John Maxwell Team, Corporate Leadership Trainer, Speaker, Facilitator for group Workshops Certified Life Coach, Entrepreneur, Anointed Prayer Warrior, Worship Leader, Minister, Singer, Song writer, Event host and dedicated friend.

In addition, she is a part of the prestigious Women Who Shape Our World, WOW Women, and Refining Women Worldwide.

Debbie earned her Bachelor's Administration degree from Brewton Parker Christian College , she is presently earning her Masters at Western Governors University.

Jelisa Cook

J elisa Raquel is a published writer, 3X award-winning journalist, pro blogger and PR Strategist. She has been writing professionally since 2005 about various topics; beauty, entertainment, lifestyle, music, and current news. Jelisa earned her Bachelor's degree from Jacksonville State University. Jelisa's work can be seen in national publication *Sheen Magazine* digital and print.

She's the creator behind women empowering brands *The Media Girls Network Inc.* and *Broadcasting Beauty Publicity*.

Jelisa combines her passion for writing, marketing, and networking together to create multiple platforms to enhance the millennial entrepreneur. Ultimately, her brands and events have attracted celebrities, influencers, and millennial entrepreneurs worldwide. Jelisa has previously interviewed stars such as, Tyler Perry, Matthew Knowles, Anthony Hamilton, Blac Chyna, Gucci Mane, Karrueche, Dominique Wilkins, En Vogue, Lil Mama, Lance Gross, Brandy, Keke Palmer and many more as an entertainment journalist.

Jelisa is the creator and founder of a new digital platform and community mediagirlsinc.com that targets female entrepreneurs and career-driven millennials focused on building careers in the media. Jelisa takes pride in connecting the dots with media, entertainment, publicity, and entrepreneurship.

The *Media Girls Network* and *Broadcasting Beauty Blog* platforms were created to enhance and close the gap between entertainment, media, and the millennial entrepreneurship experience. Media Girls on Tour platforms have held mixers, brunches, and networking socials in cities such as Atlanta, Charlotte, Detroit, and Chicago. Media Girls Network Inc. connects thousands in news media, radio media, bloggers, authors, and entrepreneurs across the globe. Featured in Rollin Out Magazine and The Voyager ATL. Currently residing in Atlanta, GA. Expect nothing but greatness from this rising serial entrepreneur.

Georgette Cunningham

Georgette wears many hats. She is a mother, life coach, Evangelist, entrepreneur, author, survivor and an anointed Woman of God. Georgette was met with tragedy early on in her life, being the survivor of sexual assault at the age of eight.

Her battle with this trauma, coupled with a urning for true love and identity sent her on a path of self destruction, with hurt manifesting itself into rebellion against her mother, and suspensions from school. At the age of fifteen, she became a mother. The suddenness of parenthood motivated Georgette to go after her destiny.

Georgette is now owner and founder of Salon Royalty LLC. Georgette has been featured in *EntreprenHer Magazine* as one of the Top 50 Inspirational Woman in the Country and currently holds a Bachelors in Theology. The founder of *Her Story Initiative*, a sisterhood for adolescents and women offers companionship, counseling and inspiration for survivors.

It is her mission to support and uplift her community, standing in the gap for others who are survivors of tremendous trauma, and bringing them into deliverance through the Lord.

Louise Davis

Louise is a devout Christian, wife, and mom of five! Currently, she is as a Strategic Planner for those who are considered 'at-risk' globally. She is a Lay Leader, and Stephen Minister with Bethel United Methodist, and active Ministry participant with Bibleway Church International.

Louise is a prayer warrior. She believes that the Saints should always 'pray without ceasing', because 'nothing is too hard for God'. Louise has received and also witnessed miracles, breakthroughs, and deliverance- in her life, and in the lives of others. Her spiritual gifts include- knowledge and wisdom of the Word of God, encouragement, teaching, ministering, and the gift of help.

Louise declares Jeremiah 29:11, to those of faith, 'For I know the plans I have for you', says the Lord, 'plans to prosper you and not to harm you, plans to give you hope and a future.'

Tameka Garrett

Tameka is the founder of Stillettos on the Pavement, author and speaker.

LaQuetia Gilliard

LaQuetia a wife and mother of two. My greatest love is the Lord and Savior Jesus Christ.

My journey began in 2008 with a strong draw to the word. I could not put it down. Every place I went, studying the word of God was what I did during every free moment I had. The more I learned the more I wanted to learn. After a while, I had so much in me that it started flowing out. No matter where I went, I shared what I was learning and studying. Where I am today started with and depends on being a habitual student of the Word.

Fast forward to 2020, and nothing has changed about being a student. However, what birthed from it was beyond my imagination – Bible Study Teacher, Blogger, Conference Speaker, Author, Mentor, Sunday School Teacher, to name a few. The more I seek Him, the more I can see and hear where He calls me.

Along with studying the Word, I also love a great cup of herbal tea, jigsaw puzzles, variety puzzles, soap making and eating out. My goal for 2020 is to rekindle my passion for the violin.

Antoinette Holman

Antoinette is a woman who has been stripped by God by incarceration, suicide of a child, been a prison wife to a man who is serving 25 to life, ostracized from family, was depressed and suicidal. bit I had an encounter with Jesus and today I am purposed, and willing to reach back and encourage ,educate and empower other people. May God continue to bless the words in my.mouth, to always edify the Body and glorify Him.

Jana Jackson

Jana is an overcomer, and a mental health advocate that is passionate about helping others.

Sharolym Jackson-Douglas

Sharolyn is married with two biological adult children and three bonus adult children and four grandchildren. I was born and raised here in Columbia, SC and a graduate of Eau Claire High School. I am a retired Lieutenant with South Carolina Department of Corrections. I own two businesses, Belleza, LLC and a Independent Beauty Consultant with Mary Kay.

Javion Woods-James

Javion is the owner of LifeEaze Virtual Assistant, and founder of More than A Mother, which is an organization that encourages women to pursue life outside of being just a mother or wife. Javion is the mother to 10 beautiful children who are her most prized possessions. Married at age 15 Javion became a young mother and wife in which she dedicated her life to in totality. Shortly after being wed, she found herself in an abusive marriage both physically and mentally. Due to her religious beliefs, she chose to stay and pray believing and hoping that one-day things would get better. Unfortunately, 8 kids later and 10 years later she realized that things would not change and that she needed to walk away, or she would end up dead. In 2009 after fighting for her life, she willed the strength to leave and try to begin the journey of finding herself and defining the life that God gave her. Choosing to survive and thrive is what she did, and she is still doing that to this day. Javion has since then received her degree in Business Management, started her own business LifeEaze VA, birthed a woman's organization, "More than a Mother", and is wed to an amazing man, Mark James Jr. She now sits on the governing board of SAVE (Standing Against Violence Everyday) which is a non-profit organization that fights domestic violence and dating abuse, and Co-Chair Vice President for the Urban League of the Upstate Project Ready. Javion believes that we all have a story and no one can tell it quite like you, live to tell it.

Nakia Morgan

Nakia is an Integrative Health Coach & Speaker. I support women over 40 to master their mindset, increase their energy & gain goal clarity. This is my purpose! I am a wife, mom and daughter.

Calotta Porterfield

Calotta is a speaker, author, and mentor that stresses the importance of having a personal and intimate relationship with God through the love and application of His word. Out of this love she is birthing D.I.V.E. (Define, Investigate, Verify and Engage) which is dedicated to enriching lives in truth through small group discussions, mentoring and media.

Tanya E. Randall

Tanya is an innovative Woman of God with a strong vision, passion and an anointing to capture the heart of people through her stunning and cutting edge display of her writings. Tanya E Randall is a 3rd Millennium African American Playwright, Producer, Director and CEO of Tanya E Randall Productions Company LLC She is also a radio personality on 94.3 WYBC FM Sunday Morning Sweet Sounds of Praise Radio Show, an entrepreneur and a full time evangelist.

She is married to her amazing husband Juane Randall and they have four young adults and seven grandchildren. Her love has always been helping people and she believes she is a brand that transforms lives through her oratory speeches, writings and love for seeing people impacted around her.

She is a humbled person called by God on one simple scripture, Romans 8:18, "For I reckon that the sufferings of this present time are not worthy to be compared with the glory which shall be revealed in us. "

Stephanie Sherer

Stephanie is a believer in walking in your purpose. Living in my year of YES! I am a current school counselor helping teens through the socio-emotional changes they experience. I am an educator by day, and a author/writer and mom by night.

Gloria Strauthers

J umping hurdles was a way of life for Gloria on her path to achieving her impossible dream. Her path to success was compounded by teen-pregnancy, domestic violence, and homelessness. It was out of her own traumatic experiences in her personal and work life, that she learned to be intentional in adding value to others. Today, she can be found intentionally adding value to others as Principle of Exodus Management & Consulting, LLC. Gloria helps organizations solve the 72% of business problems and opportunities that originates from broken processes. By building upon the 21+ years amassed through an impressive portfolio of corporate and government experiences, She creates systems, procedures, and solutions designed to ensure clients experience improved operational outcomes. Gloria is an Independent Certified John Maxwell

Team Speaker, Trainer and Coach and uses the Leadership philosophies of Dr. John C. Maxwell to pull out of others, their untapped potential and limiting beliefs holding them back from living their God-given Purpose.

Gloria is a multi-credentialed professional who specializes in Cleaning Solutions, Leadership Development, Management Consulting, and Youth programs. She is an Alumna of The University of Southern Mississippi, The Community College of the Air Force, and Tougaloo College. She is married to David Strauthers and is a resident of the State of Georgia and they have a blended family of five, and are the proud Grandparents of one Grandson.

Sherrie Truelove

Sherrie Truelove is the Founder/CEO of Faithful Transformation Ministry; a strong motivational speaker. She has received many awards for her accomplishments, dedication and commitment to God. A strong Woman of God who has experienced some of the worst trauma in life that one can imagine. This strong woman of God has learned what it means when you have been "Chosen". For a long time, she felt that God did not love her because her life had been "pure hell" since her childhood. Over the years, She learned to believe and received that God chose her to experiences all of this so that she can relate to families, children who may feel their life is over or struggle with being a single parent, foster child, a child who feel unloved, a child or parent with a disability.

She has a desire, a passion, a love to fill their hearts with unconditional love in many ways. She sees so much pain through their eyes and have so much love and warmth to give. Her positivity and sense of humor are the most valuable things about her. She has a passion to enhance and touch the lives of many families; especially women (Young and Old) to demonstrate true and unconditional love from her heart to many. Sherrie Truelove believes that God chose her to learn to cope with many of life's struggles and challenges so that she can relate to women, teens and children who feels their life is over…when it's just the beginning. A journey to destination that God has divinely created for each of us…a journey believing that "Hope" is wishing for rain…but "Faith" is carrying the umbrella. A journey toward putting life pieces back together with a true heart and purpose.

Chantal Flax-Ward

Chantal was born and raised in the British Virgin Islands to a Christian home, from a tender age, I had a sense of what it meant to spread God's word. I was always encouraged by my parents to be involved in various Church ministries; but little did I know that faith work would give me the greatest pleasure of my life

Tamika S. Washington

Tamika is a work-from-home mom who started her journey of entrepreneurship all because she needed a space to work outside of the home while feeding the need for a productive, collaborative environment to grow personally and professionally. After starting her blog and podcast, and taking a leap of faith, she and her husband created ConverSpace. Tamika's background is in education coaching, professional development, and technical writing. She is a native of Columbia, South Carolina and is married to Devin Washington. They are the proud parents of Little Miss Faith Bellamy. As an mompreneur, Tamika's motto is to live on purpose, love her kingdom assignment, and learn daily. She creates collaborative events and opportunities for women to grow personally and professionally.

Irene E. Watson

Irene is a native of Atlanta, Georgia. She is retired with dual retirement status from the United States Army and the Georgia Board of Education. As a retired U.S. Army Human Resources Management and Battalion Executive Officer, she was a major contributor in coordinating and officiating military briefings, training workshops, and medical logistics events. As a retired Business Educator, she operated as a student liaison and coordinator. She collaborated with colleagues, business owners and community leaders to develop plans for career education, vocational curricula and career exploration for students.

She is a born-again believer who loves serving people, seeing souls saved, and witnessing for the Kingdom of God. She serves as a volunteer at World Changers Church International. She has been graced to organize and spearhead ARISE Women's Fellowship. An atmosphere where women of all ages, ethnicities, occupation and education can join together in a safe place to share the love of Jesus Christ.

She has an Associate of Arts in Business Administration, Bachelor of Science in Management, and a Master of Arts in Education and Instructional Leadership. She graduated from World Changers International Bible School with an Associate of Christian Studies and is currently enrolled at Restoration Theological Seminary where she will receive a Doctorate Degree in Christian Counseling with a Minor in Life Coaching in July 2020.

She currently resides in Jonesboro, Georgia. She has three children, a son-in-law and four grandchildren. Her mother and six siblings are all located in and around the metro Atlanta.

Dr. Annette West

Annette is the founder of LivingWord International Ministry and a Holistic Wellness Life Coach/Pastoral Counselor. She resides in SC with her spouse John, retired military. They have three adult children and seven grandchildren.

God has ordained, anointed, and appointed her to assist and serve others. It has been her goal to find ways to take care of her mind, body, and spiritual relationship with the Lord. As she grows, she always seek to share and empower others, which is significant to her, because as we learn to maintain an optimal level of wellness, we are better-aligned with the things of God. She is the CEO of Jante Publishing and GinQKBoost, which specializing in ginger products and sharing on healthy ways of living in alignment with Christ. She is a self-published author of six books and hundreds of articles and devotions.

She has traveled the world sharing God's truth. Presenting biblical truth, business, leadership training for all genders and age groups. She helped start and continues to sponsor a mission school in Kakamega, E. Africa, and an orphanage in Sierra Leone, W. Africa.

One of her favorite scriptures is James 1:22 which states, "Let us not just hear the word only, but live to please the Lord."

Keywana Wright

Keywana is a native of Flint, Michigan. She is a devoted mother of one daughter, Miss Tayler Williams. Ms. Wright is a self-publisher and author of the 3 short devotional books, "Walking in God's Destiny", "Keywana's Collection of Prayers and Poems", and "31 daily prayers for the Virtuous woman". She is a motivational speaker, writer, and prayer warriors. She hosts 5 Minutes Words of Encouragement on Facebook lives on Friday's mornings. A podcast program "Good Night Prayers with Keywana Wright" on Tuesdays at 9pm.

Keywana is a Jr. Missionary and serves in various capacities at her local church as well as the community. Keywana's dream is to work and serve in full-time women's outreach ministry. She has a God-giving love for women and to help them reach their purpose in the Kingdom of God. She believes in the power of prayer. She is a witness that there is nothing impossible to him that believe.

Over the past 14 years, she has continued to work in the Human Service Field. She also has worked with domestic Violence and sexual assault victims.

She is a volunteer at Carriage Town Ministries. She encourages and uplifts the women at Carriage Town with her mentor, Minister Brittany Willingham. Keywana is also a certified life coach.

Keywana holds a Bachelor of Arts degree in Family Life Education from Spring Arbor University. She recently received a certificate in Leadership in Ministry.

Keywana's favorite bible verse is "In all thy ways acknowledge him and he shall direct thy path. Proverbs 3:6

Jennifer Gray-Wymbs

Jennifer is the Founder of GRACE High Ministries, INC. It is through GRACE High she has been able to empower and inspire teen girls and their families for greatness through mentorship and discipleship. As a teen, Jennifer battled with brokenness and abandonment that led to many defeating thoughts and behaviors.

Today, as a healed woman, her passion is for the brokenness of girls and women. Jennifer has learned that through authentic, godly relationships healing is possible and that teens and women realize their strength when a sister helps her adjust her crown. Jennifer holds over ten years of experience writing devotions and lessons for teen girls and women. As a non-fiction writer, she seeks to empower teens and women through the Word of God and real-life experiences with authenticity and grace. Jennifer has worked for over 2 decades in the mental health field and has over 3 decades of experience in youth ministry.

Jennifer lives with her husband of 28 years and their children in their south Atlanta home. She has recently returned to college to complete her degree, being an example to not only her biological children but to everyone that calls her "Mom"!

Chantea M. Williams

C hantea is a writer, speaker, and independent publisher. She is the ministry leader of *Greater Working Women Ministries,* where they strive to encourage, empower and equip women to be greater women. She is the owner of Relentless Publishing House, LLC, which serves Christian, inspirational and children book writers and assists them in self-publishing their books.

She is also a chef and enjoys baking in her free time and for the holidays. As a former teen mother at the age of 15, her motto has become, "*Giving Up Is Never An Option.*" She held on to Philippians 3:14 as her life verse and it has been her constant reminder when facing life's challenges. She firmly believes that every woman is GRACED to do something.

It has been my privilege and honor to lead the authors in this amazing collaboration. It is our heart's desire that you will be encouraged and ignited to walk in your purpose more boldly and confidently.

Are you interested in joining our next anthology?

We are looking for 15 women to join us in volume 2 of our Graced For It Devotional Series. Our topic is **Your Relationships Matter.** This will be a practical book of wisdom on the following relationships:

1. Woman's relationship with God
2. Woman's relationship with Family/Friends
3. Woman's relationship with Money

The requirements are as follows:

1. Submissions are 500 words max **(Times New Roman, 12pt, 1 ½ space, Word document)**
2. Bios are 250 words max **(Times New Roman, 12pt, 1 ½ space, Word document)**
3. Headshot
4. Website

We will start accepting submissions **November 2nd- 30th.** You will submit your words of wisdom on one of the three topics. Any submission that does not follow the above requirements will be automatically disqualified. No late submissions will be accepted.

All applicants will have a 15- minute video interview **December 1st-4th** and notified by **Monday, December 7, 2020**.

The investment for the anthology is **$197** and includes the following:

1. All publishing expenses by Relentless Publishing House, LLC (value $1,547)
2. All marketing graphics (value $500)
3. Two complimentary author books (value $40)
4. One complimentary ticket to our Graced For It Retreat 2021 (value $47)
5. One free t-shirt (value $25)
6. Private Facebook group

Your investment is due in full on **Friday, December 18, 2020 by 5:00 PM/EST**. Failure to make payment on time will automatically forfeight your spot and it will be given to the next author on the wait list. NO EXCEPTIONS!

We start **Monday, January 4, 2021**. The book will be released **May 2021**.

Sign up for our mailing list at **www.greaterwomen.com** and follow us on social media @greaterwomen for up to date information. For more information, please email us at info@greaterwomen.com.

We also have a men's version on a different topic. Follow Relentless Publishing House, LLC for more information or email info@relentlesspublishing.com.

www.ingramcontent.com/pod-product-compliance
Lightning Source LLC
Chambersburg PA
CBHW060032180426
43196CB00045B/2623